HANDBOOK

FOR THE NEW MILLENNIUM

*A Guide for your Spiritual
Growth & Development*

ALEX ANDERSON AND FRIENDS

Author: Alex Anderson
Illustrations: Arpad Csanyi
Design & Publishing: MoniQ

COPYRIGHT © 2015 by Anderson Publishing
First Paperback Edition
ISBN 978-0-9947277-0-1 (pb)
Reprinted in Victoria, BC Canada

COPYRIGHT © 1999 by Alex Anderson
First Miniature Book, Handmade Coil Bound Edition
Printed in Edmonton, AB Canada

Alex Anderson's "The Work" is prepared for publication by his niece MoniQ for release in the ArtCommons.ca shop "Anderson Publishing", an online venue dedicated to his life's work. Also available in print & digital formats at Amazon Kindle Stores.

"It is our intent with this handbook
to give some useful and simple methods
for preserving the integrity of your own
growth and understanding."

ALEX ANDERSON AND FRIENDS

CONTENTS

CONTENTS

ACKNOWLEDGMENTS

Thank you to Alex for over 25 years of courage and compassionate work as a clairvoyant medium, and thank you to his Guides in Spirit for providing the information for this handbook.

Alex was a trusted contemporary Spiritual Teacher and Mentor who was not aligned with any particular religion or tradition. He gently helped people to listen and trust in their Higher Self, find their unique path, and gain new insights and understandings of the world around us.

Thank you to Hanne, Arpad and MoniQ for collaborating in 1999 to self-publish the first handmade miniature book edition which sold out. Thank you to Dorothy for editing the Biography for the new 2015 edition.

It is with humble gratitude the handbook is available to support your unique path of growth and development.

FOREWORD

The first four parts of this handbook were written around the year 1988, and were completed about one and a half years later. The fifth part "The Afterword" (now known as Principle Practices) was composed in September of 1999.

At the time of writing the first four parts, Alex thought the words were written by him only. Years later he realized that in fact the turn of phrase and the syntax were clearly not his.

"Most of you who have known my work will be acquainted with ASA (pronounced Ā-sha) but very few of you will know that there is a group of at least five individuals that are involved in my mediumship and I find it interesting that these four files are not by the same author. I am not sure who wrote which part but I am sure that these words were not intended to grace an antique floppy disk only to be lost forever.

What I find truly interesting is that the questions answered herein are ones which have been asked more commonly of late because we are now on the threshold of, if not already in the so called New Age.

A great deal of entertaining and highly inaccurate information has been written about the New Age. The fear mongers are out there predicting the end of the world and creating cults and followings by the score. It is refreshing to note that none of that kind of thought is present in this handbook and I suspect that those who espouse such mistaken ideas will all feel a bit pressed to find a new date for our immediate destruction when we all wake up the day after our predicted demise and find that we are still here and in good health.

The nature of this handbook is more disposed to organized thought and attempts to give some means by which we might be better prepared to meet the challenges of the New Age. It also gives some idea of the general movement that is occurring and what its eventual goals are.

It is 11 years since the first writings were done and no tarnish on the information is evident. I have found over the years since my first Trance experience that even the very oldest information is still valid.

The problem with information obtained from Trance is that the channel (me) often cannot see the value in the information until much later. That is why these words have languished unused for so long that their existence had been forgotten. Or perhaps it is just the right time for them to come forth.

In future I shall invite these same entities and others to come in and write as much as they will and hopefully they will also help me to find a way to get the information out there to you, the people who need and want it."

- Alex Anderson

THE KARMIC WHEEL

THE ART OF KNOWING

THE ART OF KNOWING

Wisdom is the art of knowing the difference
between the ideas of conditioning
and the ideas of universal meaning.

It is not necessary for the mind to follow the way of wisdom in order to make its way in the Earth plane but it is needful for the mind to follow the way of wisdom if the full need and purpose of the soul is to be manifested. The need for release from the karmic wheel is not likely to become realized if the needs of the soul are not met.

We are prisoners of our own lack of insight if we do not bring forward the inner understanding which drives the progress of the soul.

The soul does not fit into the body;
therefore, we are incomplete expressions
of our full degree of knowledge.

The only way to come into a clearer understanding and more complete command of ourselves is by way of fine tuning the inner communication processes that deal with our higher selves and those of our friends and associates who are in spirit, including those who guide and teach.

The need to establish this inner communication system as part of our daily lives is growing as we progress into the New Age that is before us. This age will see the demise of 'monolinear' Karmic focus and see the establishment of many facets in the life of those who choose to be aware.

The degree of development of the soul and the physical body will have much to do with the ability of individuals who attempt to become more attuned to themselves as a universal entity.

It is not to be assumed that this will come over night or that it will be only a few who will accomplish this feat of knowing the soul's purpose. It is a process that the race itself is going through and it is part of the path of development that all are on. If the individual does not choose to expand, then the life will shrink to a much less productive and more Earth grounded view.

The need for growth is common among those who fed the pull of the New Age and wish to become part of a greater understanding.

There is no other process that has changed the nature of the human race as has the evolution back to the awareness of its place in the universal plan. There is no element of the body that is carried by the human person that has influenced the development of mankind as much as this one fact.

> The person is a soul with a body
> and not the other way around.

The case for spiritual evolution is one that the scientists of this generation are just beginning to become aware of and it will be some time yet before this awareness comes to their work.

That is not to say that the scientists are not subject to the laws of progression yet but merely, as the rest of mankind, they are not aware that their work is an outgrowth of the evolution which has been taking place in all those in the physical body.

It is inevitable that the fields of belief/religion and scientific investigation/progress will join forces. It is not possible for even the least reasonable mind to ignore the fact that there is rhyme and reason in the universe.

Human evolution has been a three point thing ever since the sojourn into matter caused the awareness of the spirit to become lost. Woman/man has sought to return to the heights of understanding and awareness that are evident to the soul between incarnations.

The incarnations themselves are expressions of the need within a soul to learn and understand some forms of energy that it does not handle well. This process once indulged in, leads to a stream of lessons and awareness's at the soul level, which are not necessarily understood from the three dimensional consciousness.

The interesting thing is that in all generations and ages of the Earth there have always been a few who have a greater sense of connectedness to all life than is true of the average personality on the Earth. Until recently, for example, the last hundred years or more, it has been assumed that there would always be just a few. Such is not the case.

This is the reason why man has been blessed with the means to communicate across distance where technically this has not been possible before in the last several thousand years and never before by all citizens of Earth.

The result has been the shifting of political balance, the changing of attitudes, the consciousness raising activities of mass media. Unfortunately the mass media has had to play the business game in such a way that its messages are often polluted by the desire of money and power.

The average person has access to many means of communication, however, and that has saved the day so far as world understanding and consciousness has been concerned. Masses of information are now available to all and it is now a focus of many to discern what information is valid and useful rather than to simply obtain information.

This confusion is leading to a revolution in the thought process of the human race that is a giant step on the road to enlightenment. For if temporal information is no longer sought after and is readily available to all then what portion of this information is of real and lasting value? The answer is that which leads to an investigation of universal truth regardless of the profession or focus of the individual.

For the first time in the history of the Earth all citizens are able to participate in expansion of understanding sufficient to sift what is the prevailing notion or conditioning of the time from that which is mundane to that which is eternal and universal in nature. The idea of the information glut is designed to snow the greedy and power hungry under while the more high minded see the path before them and come into their own empowerment.

Notice the use of the word empowerment not power.

Empowerment is the awakening of an understanding of the needs of the soul.

Power has typically meant wealth, ownership or simply control over others in the physical dimension.

This form of organization has been necessary in the past for without it the world would have been in perpetual chaos and unsuited to the development of the human as a soul driven creature.

With the advent of modern science and technology it has been possible to concentrate very thoroughly the power and control in the hands of only a few. This is no longer a suitable means for development, for the speed of evolution back toward awareness almost doubles with every decade in the present Earth experience.

This increasing speed of development has made it necessary for technology to place more control back in the hands of the everyday person for it is not possible otherwise to have development of a multifaceted multi-threaded form of learning and awareness in the race as a whole.

This is the purpose of the New Age, not the development only of extra sensory powers or of spectacular displays by just a few developed souls. The time for this has passed and the need is for the evolution of ALL to take a great leap.

THE ROLE OF MEDIUMSHIP

In the Light of Today's Needs

THE ROLE OF MEDIUMSHIP

In the Light of Today's Needs

The role of mediumship has altered significantly with the needs of the age we have entered. It is no longer needful for the majority of mediumship to be focused on the proof of survival of bodily death or the existence of communication between the physical, three dimensional realm and other forms of existence.

That is not to belittle or in any way imply that those who focus on this subject are not needed any more. It will be needed very much for those whose inquiry is of a scientific nature and for those who have not yet come to accept in any way the ideas of survival and communication. Also for those who have need of comfort there is a special kind of confirmation and affirmation that such contacts can provide.

The purpose of mediumship has, from the beginning, been to create a working link between the everyday reality we live and work in and the larger more complete universe within which it exists, for the purpose of insight and benefit.

The role of the medium varies somewhat with what the need of the time is. It is to be observed that we are facing many forms of change and crisis both as separate individuals and as whole societies.

Mediumship has begun to concentrate, therefore, more on the mental, physical and spiritual health of individuals actively seeking guidance and enlightenment. The result of this is a more immediate answering to needs and especially the need to know more about the processes and cycles of life that individuals pass through.

What, then, can we expect from mediumship today that is different from mediumship at the last turn of the century? Well, let's look first at what seems to be less prevalent.

In the earlier part of this century we were much more likely to encounter physical mediumship such as apports (items that were materialized in a closed room) tables that thumped out messages in Morse code by moving up and down, materializations (appearances of discarnates in a closed room through the aegis of a very rare and special type of Trance medium) and the independent direct voice (the voice of a spirit entity which does not use the speaking mechanism of the medium).

Mediums often worked from a deep Trance state, like Edgar Cayce, and gave information that went well beyond their conscious knowledge and ability sometimes even contradicting their own inherited beliefs. It was often seen that mediums and healers alike (both are forms of mediumship) were uneducated people who seem to have developed their abilities alone or with minimal contact with other more experienced individuals.

Many had personal visionary experiences which foreshadowed the development of the abilities that would later change their lives and the lives of others. Few of them ever became rich or even well-to-do. Some of them founded associations or movements that live on to this day. Some went on to become mystics in their own way and others were badgered until even they refuted their earlier works.

One common thing can be seen in all those who became very well known. Their work was in some way spectacular. The nature and huge amount of information and experience which they left to us is still being worked through and distilled into insight. By the nature of their spectacular work they broke through the iron clad consciousness of the European,

British and American societies with the sheer weight and force of their phenomena. The rise in the literacy rate of all these cultures led to many experiencing these phenomena through books and later through radio and TV.

As the age began to shift toward Aquarius, especially in the 50's and 60's, people began to question the status quo politically and spiritually. With the recorded works of many mediums and psychics available for examination many people became convinced of the validity of these phenomena and were hungry to know more.

Add to this, the influx of ideology from other more ancient and mystic cultures which surfaced and were accepted on the basis of the benefits of their practices (for example Yoga, meditation, Acupuncture, etc.) and you have a mindset which has shifted from the need for cold hard evidence to one that is actively seeking truth and rightness in its own way.

The solving of personal problems and dilemmas becomes inextricably involved with the enlightenment and progression of the individual.

Our focus thus has shifted from a need for proof, proof and more proof to one which is oriented to proof and then some practical guidance. The effect of this change in focus has made the private reading much more of a problem solving device than one that simply forecasts events or provides evidence and comfort.

I should state here at this point that all these needs have been addressed by mediums all along but it is the amount of energy which is spent on the different types of needs and the style of the majority of Readings that has varied.

As an example, in the last 12 of my Readings only one contained a passing on of information from a friend who had recently passed to spirit and only a portion of that Reading was devoted to the encounter. The bulk of the Reading was devoted strictly to information of the problem solving type with enough verification for the individuals receiving the Reading to feel confident in the nature of the information.

The result of this shift in emphasis is a drawing away from the more physical types of mediumship to those which rely on conscious mental processes.

The onus then is on the medium to make sure the quality of information is good and the context and meaning are clearly interpreted. It is also up to the medium and those who guide the medium to filter and verify the sources of information.

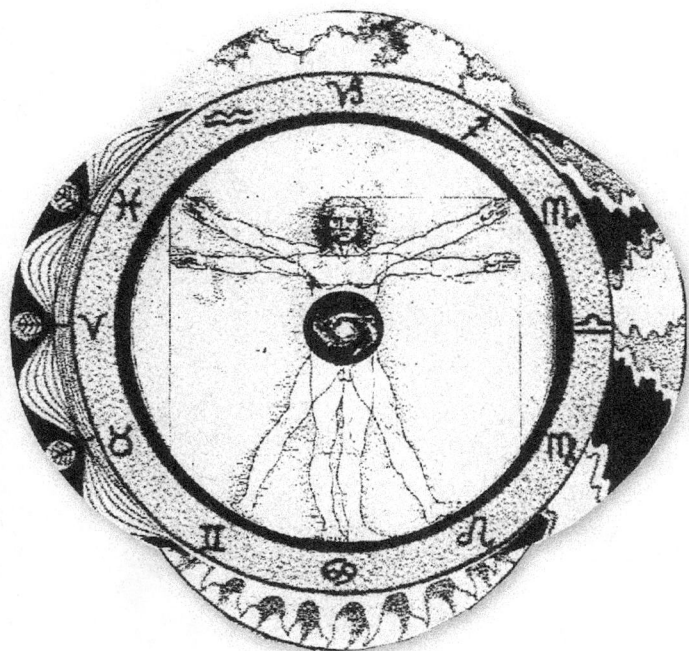

OUR CURRENT
SHIFT

OUR CURRENT SHIFT

The need to know is a fundamental driving force for the continual exploration of mankind. It is not just in the area of science that the need to know has pushed mankind to new discoveries. The spiritual side of life is calling in this age as it has been ignored for too long by the family of man in general.

There is no one race or social order that is to blame for this, it was the energy of the last age that did not lend itself well to the unfoldment of the spirit.

The age we are currently shifting into will focus in the area of the spiritual evolution of mankind and will link it once again to the realm of science and also of philosophy.

The link between man and his spiritual self is one that is so near to us that we do not see the forest for the trees. That is to say that although we are all spirit first and body second it is quite easy to forget this or "loose-consciousness" of it.

In fact there are many who are so unconscious of the spirit self that they do not believe that it exists.

This is most unfortunate for this will result in fear of the death experience. An experience that once was held sacred by many religions.

The result had been a time in man's history when the seeking after of the material power and control occurred to a frightening degree. The result of this hedonistic pursuit is the subjugation of many societies and the aggrandizement of leaders that are totalitarian in nature.

The resulting loss of freedom and the ability to creatively address the problems of technology and the literal basic needs of masses of population have created great disparity between types of civilization. The erosion of the principal of freedom which is an intrinsic part of the democratic process has led to enormous bureaucracies and financial troubles for the leading countries. These difficulties will not go away until the responsibility of the individual as a part of the whole process has come home to all societies.

There are many societies that cling to old outmoded ways of doing things simply because it is their custom.

There must therefore, come a cleaning
of the house of man. That is what
the "New Age" is all about.

It is true that this age will bring enlightenment as to the universal truths and laws. It is also true that many will find they have abilities that confound the science of the day. But the single most emphatic truth of the situation is that there will be a complete change in the way that countries are governed and in the way that the average person relates to that government.

The process of the change will be slow at first but will accelerate as the next century opens up more understanding of the laws of both the spiritual and scientific worlds. The problems that we face today with respect to the environment reflect the attitude with which mankind has lived the last age.

The way must be opened for the psychic and creative part of man to fill in the blanks that are now emerging in the way that we address the environment. This mirror is important because it reflects the inner condition of the family of man and shows clearly that there is much to clean up and to change.

Many who have romanticized about the "New Age" have seen it as a panacea for the ills of mankind and a time in which all will be resolved into a "one big happy family" situation. Nothing could be further from the truth.

This age and especially the beginning of it will be filled with turmoil and these will be societal as well as the literal "Earth changes" that have been foreseen by many psychics who have peered into the future and felt the shimmering, energetic nature of the future.

This age will begin by witnessing the fall of many of the institutions that have endured for a long time. It will also see a dying out of those societies which cling to rituals that are not up to the expanded and more enlightened potential of the race as a whole. These societies will simply dwindle in number or be absorbed into more progressive cultures which are recognizably more advanced than their old ones are.

Although there is much that will die away and become part of history, it would be well for mankind to preserve the history and pageantry of bygone days as a reminder of where they have come from.

Technology is now present in the Earth plane that will make it possible for not only the preservation of history but also to probe further back into the stay of man upon this planet and to find out more about the civilizations that have existed in the past. It is unfortunate, however, that the furthest reaches of man's history will remain a guess. Something that those who gain access to past life will have a clearer view of than the scientist and the historians will ever find in hard evidence.

Considering the Psychic

It is true that there has always been the psychic in our midst that has seen the future and who know of what has passed without ever having been there. How they obtain this information is not the subject of this piece of writing. It is sufficient to know that they have always existed and that they always will. It is thanks to them that we know as much of things to come as we do. (I speak as though I am a resident of Earth at this time, which I am not.)

The function of the psychic is to create reasonable doubt of the methods we use in living our lives and to suggest alternatives that might be practicable or more complete than the picture we have seen to date.

The psychic is not only one who sees but one who brings healing, counsel and comfort to those who have not the same abilities or who have not developed the abilities they have. The psychic is often a strange character. They propound fantastic theories, give information regarding causes and events, and bring into the three dimensional plane energies for healing that cannot be measured directly or sometimes even felt.

They often expound principles and wisdom that they themselves do not show when they are "not working" and that is because they are human beings just like everyone else and subject to all the ills and frailties that we are all heir to.

The fact that their knowledge of the universe is greater when they are connected or in a working mode is not to be wondered at, what else would be the source of their knowledge but the universe itself and those beings in it who are greater than we and have greater insight. In fact we ourselves are greater than we know because we have not got full consciousness of what we are at the spirit level of existence. There is much conjecture about what life without a body is like but there is no room here for a discussion of such conjectures. They are just simply too numerous.

The interconnectedness of woman/man with her/his environment is an unexplored realm by and large. Her/his relationship to the rest of the race is only guessed at so far. These are the things which the New Age will investigate.

The energy of the New Age is not one which will magically bring all things together in peace but one where the much needed investigation into the reality of the spiritual life will come into focus. It is, therefore up to each of us to explore as much as we are able to and to sift the truth from the fiction and fancy for there is much truth to find.

I wish you all well on your journey and hope that this discourse will have the effect of both encouraging you and cautioning you against the danger of complacent acceptance.

MEDITATION

MEDITATION

The inner experience is a mystical one that is not easy to describe, it contains the knowledge of past events and the seeds of future events and yet is not removed or separate from our reality.

We have a vast reservoir of knowledge at our disposal and yet we make relatively little use of it. It is also the area where we interact with the mass consciousness of our society and that of the world.

The course of meditation will take you away from normal reality in gradual but purposeful steps.

Meditation is the key to unlocking
the untapped reservoir and opening
the mind to new principles and laws
that are not immediately evident
to the fully waking mind.

The first of these steps is to address the constant chattering of the ego mind and its persistent voice which questions the current perception only lightly and tends to refer far too much to the past and the future.

The result is the rising to consciousness of memories that are related to the sojourn in the Earth and especially those events and times when we formed beliefs, behaviour patterns, fears, likes, dislikes, and a host of other mental and psychological structures that make up ourselves and our social conditioning.

It is not always necessary to understand what exactly happened when we review these things but it is helpful to understand that the recurring pattern in meditation is to become aware of these things in a conscious manner and to release them. The resulting release of energy is then useful in forming new patterns and behaviors that will result in a condition of growth.

Many of these things are so much a feeling experience that it is difficult or impossible to get the experience into words. That is, alas, a function of having a language that is not equipped to describe such things.

CAUTION

GROWTH
IN PROGRESS
PROCEED
WITH CARE

PRINCIPLE
PRACTICES

PRINCIPLE PRACTICES

The Afterword

It is in the best interest of the reader to note that Much development of the channel through which we speak and write has occurred. We are happy that these older files have been found and are at last in use. It was necessary that the channel saw the value of these writings for he is a most exacting individual and it would not have been possible to persuade him to do anything with this information if had he not been certain there was value in it.

Our work, speaking collectively, has been most enlightening to us as well as to our Alexander. We are all individuals who have lived in various times in the Earth plane but we have never had the type and variety of technological intricacies to deal with that you currently have in the Earth plane. This complicates the way of life more than we had believed possible.

You may all be proud of yourselves because merely to survive in such a world is more of an accomplishment than you know. It is also, however, a perfect example of one of our favourite concepts.

Keep everything as simple as you possibly can.

The energy of the New Age is becoming more entrenched and many of those in the Earth plane are indulging in one of humanity's favourite pastimes; panic!

The shifting of energy is enough for those who are balanced to contend with. For those who are not very well balanced it is proving to cause more trouble than is immediately visible.

Even for those who purport to be channels of information it is necessary for them to aim for stability first and let all else come second to that aim. When this is not done, the information becomes scrabbled and confused and mistaken concepts may arise.

If there has been one difficulty that the shift in the nature of mediumship has created it is this. The medium has more of a role in the interpretation of the information.

It is therefore extremely important they learn how not to interfere with or embellish the information as it is given to them.

We are not here to be critical of others or deride other works of mediumship but we must acknowledge that this difficulty does exist. It is also our aim to help give some means by which the truth might be quickly sifted from that which is unnecessary. (I think I am making our channel nervous. This is not a bad thing for it is important that he know we watch him almost as much as he watches us and he usually does his best work under pressure. He has less time to argue that way.)

For those of you who are not familiar with the concept of guides we will first explain briefly.

All those who are incarnate in the Earth plane have with them an entity in spirit who is there by agreement for the purpose of helping them through their sojourn in the Earth plane.

We have many duties but one that is very useful is the ability to carry requests or what some of you call prayers to others who can help resolve problems.

We also can help in a more subtle way by giving a sense of confirmation or denial of information that you are being given either in book form or in a class.

It is to be understood that we help on a very individual basis, and what is not useful to you now may in fact be useful to you at some time in the future when your understanding is more complete.

Therefore this is a caution to not become closed to information.

BEST PRACTICES

A guide for your daily practice.

7 simple methods to protect yourself and to sift Truth from the unnecessary.

First, before you read or perhaps even enter a place where information is available, ask those in spirit to protect you and help you to see that which is truth and good knowledge for you to absorb or incorporate into your thinking.

Second, when reading or listening to a talk, watch for unrelated truths which are brought into the information in order to lend credibility to the information which is being propounded. (This is an old propaganda method, one which was used extensively by Tokyo Rose during the war to confuse the issue and weaken the personal defenses of the opposing military.)

Thirdly, watch for information that is poorly linked or seems to be unrelated to the main topic, or is simply given in a way which appears to be deliberately unclear.

Fourth, watch for information that is inclined to make you feel as if you are less skilled, uneducated or missing the so called real truth.

Five, watch for those who either in their writings or in their lectures appears to be trying to create a following or a power structure.

Six, keep in mind that if an idea seems too weird, far out or fantastic, it probably is and you should use caution in dealing with it. That is not to say that we sanction closed mindedness in any form.

Seven, know that you are valuable and have your own path of progression and indeed your own brand of wisdom and understanding. Anything which tends to belittle this or try to take this away from you or makes you less than in any way is highly suspect.

All or any of these previous methods
are clues that you should be questioning
the validity and depth of the
information in question.

Some of you may feel that these seven principles throw doubt on even broadly accepted religions of the day. This may be, but it really serves to point out where the meddling of those with other agendas is present. In other words, who changed the original information, when and why?

It is our intent with this Handbook, to give some useful and simple methods for preserving the integrity of your own growth and understanding. We do not all have the same path to tread and therefore we must have principles that can be applied across a broad range of endeavours.

It may be your lot to pursue the path of psychic development for use as a profession or it may simply be that you are bound in this life only to further your own understanding and help those close to you do the same.

There are varying degrees of complexity in each life path and you are the one that is central to your development and progress.

We hope you enjoy the Handbook and look forward to a time when we will be able to provide you with a more complete work, which will have greater detail and more varied subject matter. (We intend to keep our channel very busy for a while.)

"Please accept our love and such
blessings as we may be able
to call upon you."

ASA, MICHAEL, GARAMONDE
AND THE CREW

AUTHORS NOTE

"None of this book is mine. This entire book is theirs (The Guides). I feel much better having finally agreed to do this and the other future projects I am aware of. I hope you will find the information and opinions useful.

It has always been the goal of The Guides to make us think and think. They've accomplished this here."

Sincerely,

Alex Anderson
1949 – 2004

BIOGRAPHY

About the Author

Alex Anderson, clairvoyant medium, was born in
Edmonton, Alberta in November of 1949. He lived in
the downtown core for his first 19 years and came to
know and like a variety of people from a variety of
cultures and lifestyles.

49

People and their ways were always of interest to Alex and in his life he held many people oriented occupations ranging from a brief sojourn as a short order cook to a student of psychiatric nursing.

It was not his intention, however, to pursue a career as a psychic. It was his contention that this occurred more by fortune than management.

In his early thirties he sat with a development circle in a Spiritualist church and later served briefly as a medium in their Message services. This organization also exposed him to developed, experienced mediums whose work was of a high caliber. Since that time he attempted to pursue a career path that fit the description of ordinary but has always been drawn back to using his gifts and wits on behalf of Spirit and those who seek help from them.

The greater portion of his psychic work occurred after 1984. "The Work", as he called it, consisted mainly of private Readings but there were also development circles that he hosted and there was the development of the ability to bring information through while in a form of Trance. That is how this book was obtained and that is how his Guides have been able, on occasion, to address large groups of people. This has produced some interesting information and insights into what is occurring during this time of intense change and development of the Human Race.

In future there will be more information obtained in the form of written material and Alex hoped to compile these into larger works to be more complete in their organization and depth of information. There is also the information from the public Trance sessions which has been preserved and which will be brought forward and assembled into interesting and useful works.

It may seem a long time from the early 80's to the present moment but one of the issues that was very dear to Alex was quality. He must be convinced of the quality of "The Work" or he would not have proceeded. He gave most of the credit for his work to "The Guides" and maintains that without their greater insight and more intense energy none of this would be possible.

Over a 25 year career as a clairvoyant medium Alex offered private Readings to his many cherished clients near and far, most of whom lived on Vancouver Island, British Columbia and in Edmonton, Alberta.

Alex was a trusted contemporary Spiritual Teacher and Mentor who was not aligned with any particular religion or tradition, although he had a strong association with Tibet. He gently helped people to listen and trust in their Higher Self, find their unique path, and gain new insights and understandings in the world around us. He provided classes in spiritual development; gave talks at spiritual centres, book stores and psychic events; and Alex channeled valuable information for private Readings and public Trance Sessions that will surely continue to resonate.

Re-reading Alex's writings and listening to his audio recordings over again makes one aware of how the information provided over the years is timeless and contains layers of insights and understandings yet to be discovered.

Alex Anderson spent his last years in Victoria, British Columbia with close family and friends. In the fall of 2004 he passed away too soon at the age of 55.

Alex is greatly missed.

PUBLISHERS NOTE

"After accomplishing a 15 year healing journey the importance of 'The Work' has returned along with my Uncle Alex's 2002 personal request to continue his life's work and ensure it is published and made available for those ready to move forward."

For the Highest Good,

- MoniQ

To find "The Work" in print & digital format by Alex Anderson and Friends; including written Teachings and audio recordings of Trance Sessions & Group Meditations go to:

ArtCommons.ca Shop: Anderson Publishing
and Amazon Kindle Stores.

For more information on Alex Anderson, and for a more comprehensive selection and online educational learnings to come, contact the publisher online at:

www.ArtCommons.ca/AndersonPublishing